ideas
centre
group

Book 1

Thinking Money Down the Drain

Notes

Thinking Money
Down the Drain
Contents

Notes

Introducing
Creativity and Innovation

The future survival of organisations will depend on an ability to break with deeply ingrained habits, rewarding those that can overcome tradition and convention to release the potential of "what might be". The threats posed by "more of the same" are enormous, and the business community is littered with examples of organisations that were once prosperous, based upon hugely successful models but now struggling or even closing down as the world around them is changing.

Notes

> **"It is not necessary to change: survival is not compulsory"**
> *(W Edwards Demming)*

The world around us is changing at an ever increasing pace – and as a consequence it is exploding with opportunity providing those with agility, flexibility and freedom of mind with the ability to transform both themselves and their organisations.

However, as individuals and collectively within organisations, we all make sense of the world around us by looking backwards, understanding what has gone before, and then using this to determine our actions moving forward. All of our thinking, decision-making and therefore our behaviours are determined by what we see in the rear-view mirror. We draw upon our learning, our experiences, our accumulated know-how, and then force-fit the reality into our historic models.

This force-fit process then ensures decisions which are consistent with our past experiences – constraining us to develop our own little worlds in which everything behaves in a self-consistent manner, and traditional thinking is thus established. We are perfectly safe and secure within this world, and for the vast majority of the time it serves us well. But if we allow ourselves to become trapped within the atmosphere of convention, we as individuals, and therefore the organisations that we work for, will inevitably get left behind; there is an ever-widening gap between the world of "what is" and the universe of "what might be".

Notes

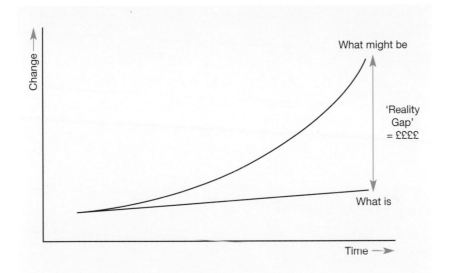

Figure 1.1: The Reality Gap – representing a massive prize for those that develop an understanding of "break-though thinking"

The prize that awaits those that take time to understand the thinking processes is tremendous. Based on current practice alone (i.e. no product or market innovation), there is ample published evidence to suggest that organisations are **wasting up to 30% of their costs** – and perhaps **as high as 50% in the service sector**, simply because of the way that they think! Even if this is over-stating the situation in an organisation by a factor of two, and supposing that we can then only eliminate half of the available waste, then we are still identifying a boost to the bottom line of 7.5% - 12.5% of revenues.

Notes

We simply **must** find ways of challenging these patterns of behaviour, to free up our thinking, to generate novel and useful (i.e. creative) ideas that drive innovation and transform organisations – shrinking the "reality gap".

Organisations have long understood the importance of challenging the internal practices, and Continuous Improvement programmes have become essential to retaining a competitive position within the market. However, such programmes are bound by in-house traditions – or culture; invisible boundaries to thinking are defined, beyond which one is simply unable to go. Such self-limiting beliefs result in a major block to progress; what we need is *breakthrough thinking*.

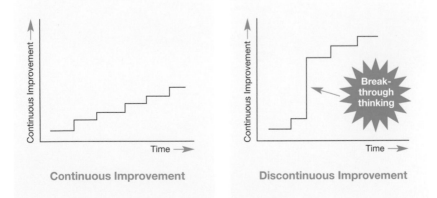

Figure 1.2: Continuous and Discontinuous Improvement.

Notes

> *"Whether you think you can, or you think you can't*
> *– you're right"*
> (Henry Ford)

Continuous Improvement is concerned with **doing the same things better**, led from the top of an organisation but actually delivered at the grass roots i.e. *bottom-up*; *Discontinuous Improvement*, by contrast, focuses on the addition of occasional step changes in performance, representing breakthroughs in thinking and to be successful must be delivered *top-down* i.e. they are a responsibility of management. Management are in a unique position; responsible for leadership and the development of outstanding performance, they are also privileged to be exposed to a range of external influences to provoke fresh thinking, and have the freedom to consider new ways of working that may *transform* operations. Those with their heads buried in the day-to-day detail – operational staff – will certainly be able to *contribute* to the breakthrough process, but are less likely to take the responsibility for such a transformation (potentially threatening their position within the organisation... although such individuals should surely be more likely to be promoted than dismissed!).

This breakthrough process is all about **thinking differently**, challenging convention and tradition, being **creative and innovative**. The understanding of these concepts is critically important to future success of organisations of all types.

Notes

Creativity

The terms *creativity* and *innovation* are often used and too often little understood. Every organisation claims to be innovative if only to suggest a level of credibility, and it is becoming increasingly fashionable to talk about creativity. However – it is easy to claim, and far less easy to deliver. Such delivery can only be produced in a consistent manner if these terms are clearly understood... by the whole organisation.

The term *"creative"* has negative connotations for many, referring to individuals that are not quite in touch with the "real world". Creative types are often considered to be difficult to manage, unfocused, unpredictable, liable to do real damage if exposed alone to customers or suppliers! This is not a good fit with the majority of organisations, and yet the same organisations recognise the need to be creative to compete or even exist in an increasingly challenging world. Without an understanding of the term *creativity*, it is difficult if not impossible to square the circle.

Cutting through the swathes of publications on the subject, here is a simple definition:

Creativity: The generation of ideas which are <u>both</u> novel *and* useful

The combination of novelty *and* usefulness is key. The generation of ideas that are simply useful, but not novel, is vital... but *not* creative. Indeed, the vast majority of issues are best addressed by the rapid, logical generation of useful ideas – a process which is dominated by the left-side of the brain (see Chapter 2), based upon tradition and convention.

Notes

Education in the Western world is largely focused on the development of this left-brain thinking; written examinations test mechanistic approaches to problem solving with classic patterns taught and (hopefully!) learnt, to be regurgitated and applied within a hushed exam environment. Organisations need this skill, with complicated situations and time pressures that favour those with highly developed logical thinking. Those that show exceptional skills in problem solving are typically those that get promoted. There is simply no time to sit back and ruminate, to ponder the situation.

Yet these are the core behaviours for creativity – representing an ability to take time and reflect, looking at things from different perspectives, making new connections to spark fresh ideas. If traditional left-brain thinking involves **doing things better**, then creative thinking is all about **doing things differently**, tapping into the right side of the brain. *Novelty* is derived from breaking with tradition – which instantly exposes an associated risk, as novelty represents an acute form of change which challenges an organisation's real desire to break the mould. This may result in the rejection of a truly creative idea, or at least a reluctance to act. More on this later (Chapter 3).

Clearly, it is equally *not* creative to generate ideas that are both novel and *useless*. However, do note that many creative problem solving techniques are based upon a two-stage process;

First   suspending all judgement and generating an idea which is novel and useless (it would indeed solve the problem, if only it were possible and/or legal and/or ethical and/or moral to implement);

Second   protecting the novelty factor but converting the useless into useful, gradually bringing judgement back into the solution.

Notes

We will explore this process in more depth in Book 2, but a key point to note here is practically how difficult it is to undertake the *alternative* (reversed) two-stage process – taking a simply useful idea and then adding in novelty; the logical left-brain is not at all comfortable with novelty (which is at odds with the conventional thinking), and will effectively protect "useful" from the threats presented by "novelty", which is then rejected.

A Culture of Creativity

With this simple clarity of understanding of the concept of Creativity, what proportion of the staff within your organisation would you wish to be able to generate ideas that are both novel and useful?

Surely all of them. Creativity is then less to do with quirky individuals to be kept under control, or the attendance at a whacky weekend workshop on creativity techniques which will never be used in anger again, but more to do with the very *culture* of the organisation. It is then not enough for a few creative types to be dotted through the functional areas, but for *everyone* to embrace a new philosophy, and a new approach that understands what it means to "think differently". Note that this *does not* imply the promotion of a chaotic approach to processes, or the demotion of traditional left-brain thinking. The vast majority of problems will still demand quick, logical, problem solving skills, drawing upon past experience and knowledge of "how we do things round here"; but this new culture is also excited about the prospects of *doing things differently*, in ways that challenge the old beliefs and lead to major step changes in performance.

Innovation

In promoting the act of doing things differently, the emphasis must lie on the word **doing**. For the vast majority of organisations, the process of generating ideas (whether novel or

Notes

not) is simply a waste of time unless those ideas are then implemented and integrated within the regular operations. Hence the very simple definition:

Innovation: Making money/adding value from creativity

Innovation is a **doing** thing – clearly distinct from creativity (associated with *idea generation*). The blocks to creativity sit within the minds of individuals, and are associated with the way that we think; innovation, by contrast, is all about **implementation**, involving structures and processes, and the associated blocks then typically sit at an *organisational* or *cultural* level.

What's the Problem?

It is worth noting at this early stage that this book may refer to both "problems" and "issues" interchangeably – but with a strong preference for the term "opportunities". Problems and issues are commonly negative, associated with things going wrong, and it is certainly true that creativity has a role to play in this context. Where the "problem" is immediate, demanding a decision and action on a rapid timescale, then left-brain thinking (rapid, logical) will certainly be at the forefront. However, most (…all?) organisations suffer from deep-seated, recurring problems, reluctantly tolerated and then systematically incorporated within the processes, and addressed through a series of workarounds or "fixes" which fail to address the core problem, but which compensate in some way – albeit at a consequential cost to the organisation.

The term "opportunities" should probably be preferred as it embraces both *doing things better* _and_ *doing things differently*. Sure, breakthrough thinking is required to overcome the deep-seated problems highlighted above, but the same is also required to find ways

Notes

to provide access to truly outstanding performance – blocked from view due to traditional thinking which then limits behaviours and associated actions.

Structure of this book

Blockages to Creativity:

Chapter 2: **The Thinking Process**

Chapter 3: **The Brain as a Patterning System**

Chapter 4: **Mind Set**

This book is intended to help in the understanding of the blockages to our thinking and consequential behaviours that confine us to the world of "what is", that operate within all of our minds. Whilst we cannot make these blockages disappear, by understanding them we can explore tactics, tricks and techniques to overcome them, and then to release the creativity within *everyone*.

This book (**Book 1**) will focus on the underlying issues that block the creative process;

Book 2 (An Introduction to Creative Problem Solving Techniques) will introduce mechanisms to overcome those blockages and to embed new behaviours within the organisation;

Book 3 (The Magic of Creative Facilitation) will explain the critical role played by the facilitator within the process of problem solving, distilling the magic and driving new thinking.

Notes

Blockage 1:
The Thinking Process

First and second stage thinking

There is a vast amount of research that has been undertaken which explores the thinking process, but essentially *thinking* may be divided up into **first** and **second** stage processes (Edward de Bono introduced the alternative terms *lateral* thinking and *vertical* thinking respectively). Here is the central blockage; **we are all massively biased towards second stage thinking**. This is the area of thinking through which problems are solved or issues addressed. It is fundamentally action-oriented. Second stage thinking is the process by which we:

Notes

Step 1: gather information relating to the issue;

Step 2: process that information; and then

Step 3: generate an outcome, or perhaps an action.

It is a logical, quick process – and 99%+ of the time it is just what we need. The majority of educational systems around the world are focused on this *second stage* thinking. Students are trained to identify key information, which is then processed to generate a solution to a problem. If the student can remember equations or rules of thumb, simply pick the relevant information from the exam question and drop it into the process; turn the handle, and out pops the answer.

Probably the best example of a second stage thinking process is a computer. The user identifies inputs (i.e. the data to be processed) and selects a programme to be run. The programme has already been set to operate in a defined way, using algorithms or equations to crunch the data, to generate a single solution. It is the process of acting upon the data to generate a solution that is second stage thinking.

It is also a process which is driven by the left hand side of the brain. The majority of the physical mass of the brain divides nicely into two hemispheres, left and right, and science has spent considerable effort over the last 75 years trying to understand the functioning within each. Whilst phenomenal amounts are still to be learnt, what has become clear is that the transfer of information within each hemisphere is quite different.

Within the left side of the brain, the *neurons* through which information is transmitted are short, quick-firing, and massively interconnected through structures referred to as

Notes

dendrites. Information is processed rapidly, and the existing interconnections predetermine logical pathways which define the manner in which processing takes place. The second-stage process is driven by the left-brain.

Although the left-brain may be driven by logic, it is precisely this logic that is constrained by past experience via previously formed patterns of connecting neurons which now determine our understanding and subsequent analysis of the issue. Creativity is fundamentally lost precisely because we rush in with our conventional thinking, applying *perceived* logic to quickly generate a solution; always useful, but seldom novel. **First stage thinking**, by contrast, is **not about <u>solving</u> the problem,** but **about <u>exploring</u> the problem**… before then going on to solve it using second stage thinking.

First stage processes can be understood as right-brain thinking; here the neurons are longer but less connected. Right-brain thinking is therefore associated with a degree of patience, exploring possible new connections that may or may not lead to a satisfactory outcome. There is less preconditioning, generating new thought processes from which fresh understanding might emerge. Understanding the right-brain provides a key to breakthrough thinking.

Reminder: creativity = the generation of ideas that are both novel <u>and</u> useful ideas

Second stage thinking alone tends to generate useful ideas which are not novel. First stage thinking is all about finding new angles – the right-brain process, taking time, building within the subconscious… and a practice which we neglect. The conscious self takes over when focusing on a problem, engaging directly with the left brain – logical, process-driven, and fast; if the right brain attempts to intrude, reflecting and ruminating and generally taking time, then the impatience of the left brain takes over – and quickly generates a useful idea, dispelling any potential novelty.

Notes

First stage thinking should take place *prior* to the processing of the data if creativity is to be engaged. It is the process of **exploring the problem** or the opportunity, but not trying to solve it. It involves consideration of the available data from a range of angles, trying to find another way of defining or **reframing** the problem or opportunity.

To think differently, we need to spend time *resisting* the temptation to rush into solving problems, spending time thinking about and exploring them first. A simple example of both first and second stage thinking will demonstrate the difference between the two:

> **Example: First and Second Stage Thinking**
> *Consider a tournament with 91 competitors in a simple knock-out format.*
> *How many games are played through to and including the final?*

In this example, the tendency is to leap into second stage thinking – immediately working towards a solution. One starts with the classical representation of the various rounds of the tournament, with the number of games halving for successive rounds... or doubling if you prefer to work backwards from the final. But with a big, odd number to start with this is difficult. There must be at least one bye (a "walk-through", not a game), but how many in total?

We grab the *information* (91 competitors) and then we *process* it (tournament format, half then half then half again etc.), and hopefully the *answer* will emerge:

 **91 competitors +** 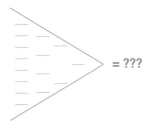 **= ???**

Notes

However, the bycs confuse the processing, and somewhat get in the way; unless we can figure out a solution to this issue quickly, then the impatience of the left-brain takes over and stops the process. We switch off, and conclude that it is too hard.

If you stick with it, then it is likely that you merely use the same second-stage process, but think *harder* about it! The answer is in there, we just need to get it!!

By contrast, a pure first stage thinking approach can massively simplify the problem – see below.

The power of first stage thinking!
So to try and solve the problem creatively; look at it from different angles, to try and reframe the problem in some way:

How many losers are there in each game played?
How many losers are there in the entre tournament?

With this insight into the problem (all to do with understanding, nothing to do with solving... yet), now is the time to move into second stage thinking. If there is 1 loser for each game played and 90 losers in the entire tournament, then how many games are played?

This first stage thinking provides access to a simple generic solution: if there are N teams in such a tournament, there will be N-1 games played – regardless of the value of N. Too simple to be true? Try the method out for 2 teams, and 8 teams.

Just a party trick? No, this major focus on second stage thinking has serious applications within the organisational context. Faced with issues, meetings are often convened to find a fresh approach. Little, if any, time is spent trying to look at the problem from different

Notes

angles. Time pressures exist, so the temptation to lunge into second stage thinking is irresistible. Individuals will look at past experience, and invent rules and approaches based upon this experience to help to find a solution.

Unfortunately, this same dash for second stage thinking is used when we attempt to think of new products or service ideas, new delivery processes and any other aspects of the business model.

Puzzle versus Problem

We have seen how first stage thinking can dramatically simplify the process of problem solving. Now, the example above is not typical of a business issue – in that it has a single, unique correct answer; in short, it is a "puzzle". By contrast, in business there are rarely unique answers to problems, but rather an infinite spectrum of solutions that range from good to bad:

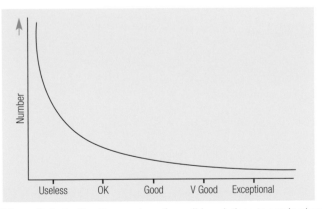

Figure 2.1: Schematic indicating the number of possible solutions to any business issue

Presented with a problem, most managers will be able to generate an idea which is reasonably useful on this graphical representation. However, if dominated by second stage

Notes

thinking, traditional thought processes will effectively restrict access to certain parts of the spectrum of solutions in Figure 2.1, and it is then surely unlikely that the _very best_ solutions will be identified – losing potential benefit/advantage.

A little time invested in first stage thinking can transform the process and provide access to alternative interpretations of the problem which are therefore inherently _novel_ – a prerequisite for creativity. By investing time in problem exploration, it is then possible to de-restrict access to parts of the spectrum of solutions in Figure 2.1 (previous page), thus widening the choice and increasing the potential for creativity.

As you can see, the thinking process itself, ingrained by the education system, presents a major block to creativity. Once aware, you will see numerous examples of this dramatic tendency to dive into problem solving, rather than exploring the problem first. As someone starts to explain an issue, the brain will immediately engage in trying to identify the key bits of information, piecing them together to understand the core mechanisms, and then to start solving it. By the time the issue is fully explained, there is an idea ready formulated, and keen to get out!

We need assistance to manage this habit to "solve" rather than first "understand and explore" an issue, and there are many techniques that can be used to assist (See Book 2: An _Introduction to Creative Problem Solving Techniques_).

An Issue of problem definition

It is commonly the case that organisations identify the "Problem as Defined" (a simple top level definition of the problem to be addressed), and then leap into problem solving mode (i.e. _second stage thinking_). We all understand the problem, so what's the point of spending time on it, when it is the solutions that we really want to get at (... the "exciting bit")? But this top level problem is commonly crudely defined, inaccurate and frequently combining

Notes

a number of aspects into a single definition. These are the problems that won't go away – which is not surprising, since these "nested" problems are addressed by the pursuit of a single "silver bullet" solution; we latch on to an idea that should solve the problem, only to discover that it instantly springs back at us – not surprising, as the chances of finding a single solution for such "nested" problems (expressed as a single issue) are somewhat remote/negligible/non-existent!

For example, take the simple problem definition that will resonate within many organisations:

How can we improve communication within the organisation?

This sloppy top level problem definition is inevitably representative of many lower level sub-problems:

How can we...   **improve the use of e-mail?**
keep staff informed?
keep staff informed of organisational developments?
keep staff informed of relevant changes within the sector?
keep staff informed of customer feedback?
improve verbal communication?
improve the use of the intranet?
improve communication with the sales team?
improve communication with the shop floor?
improve communication between project teams in research?
improve communication between sites?
etc.

The chances of a problem solving exercise coming up with a solution to address all of the above? Zero. There is no silver bullet. Second stage thinking will get us nowhere.

Notes

The creative problem solving cycle

So, to encourage and prioritise *first stage* thinking, we must engage the services of the first part of the Creative Problem Solving Cycle, focusing on Problem Exploration:

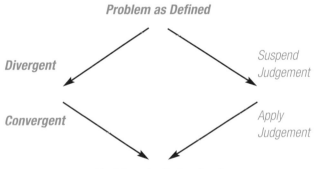

Figure 2.2: Problem Exploration within the Creative Problem Solving Cycle

We start with the **Problem as Defined**. This is a simple top-level definition of the issue at hand, probably starting with "How can..." or some such construction. Then...

- The Facilitator will introduce a technique (see Book 2) to provoke a process of *divergent thinking*, suspending judgement, during which "anything goes".
- This is then followed by a process of *convergent thinking*, during which judgement is gently and progressively brought back onto the table.
- The result is a freshly defined problem with much greater consideration and clarity, and which, through the process, is fully understood by all in the Problem Solving Group i.e. the "Problem as Understood". This process is commonly referred to as **re-framing** the problem.

The whole process can be completed within 20 minutes – time well-spent.

Notes

Blockage 2:
Patterning Systems

Pattern recognition: a neat data processing trick

The brain is bombarded with a huge array of information on a continuous basis. Take just *one* of our senses – sight: every component of the elements that make up our vision contains a vast amount of pixelated detail – position, colour, contrast, brightness etc. We use this data to recognise objects, calculate relative positions, make judgements about movements, determine our reactions... and all of this is (literally) a moving object, as our eyes constantly flicker, demanding the continuous re-processing of all data.

Notes

Simultaneously, the other four senses (sound, smell, taste, touch) are feeding the brain with a torrent of data. Using standard technology, if the brain tried to analyse each and every individual data point in real time, it would surely shut down! But the brain converts this data into information that our brains can process in real time – with none of the "buffering" delays that we are now so unfortunately familiar via our computers.

In order to cope with this mass of data, the brain has developed a "cheat"; the brain simply groups the information into patterns, and then operates on these rather than detailed data that makes up those patterns. Whilst the *conscious* brain can famously "hold" a maximum of approximately 7 items at any one time, it is the *subconscious* brain that is in control of our patterning.

Imagine the brain to contain (metaphorically!) a huge filing cabinet of such patterns, collected painstakingly over the years, and neatly filed and indexed, ready to be called upon as required. As data is presented, the subconscious brain flicks through the cabinet to find the patterns that it can match to the incoming data – to see if it has been presented before. Once a matching pattern is located from the cabinet, and provided that it does not represent a threat which demands conscious action, then the detailed data can be ignored.

Figure 3.1:
The metaphorical pattern
store in the brain – all
neatly filed and indexed

Notes

This "pattern matching" — comparing real-time data from our senses with the stored patterns within our brains — is largely handled by the subconscious brain. The comparison process takes less than a millisecond to complete — unless, of course, there is no pattern previously stored. Under such circumstances the brain will *consciously* process the newly presented information, understanding what it can from the detailed data presented, and then store it away for future comparison. In simple terms, and for example, we do this every time we meet someone new — all going on in the background, managed by the ever-active subconscious brain.

Imagine walking into a room full of people. Those that you have met before, you instantly pick out through the pattern matching process. As you look around the room the rest of the people are being scanned and compared with your stored images; if no match is identified, you pass on — disinterested. Now, however, you get into conversation with someone — demanding a conscious effort to engage. Your subconscious is already busy at work, scanning the new person into the filing system, and indexing them under various appropriate headings for easy access in the future.

If we later bump into that individual in a fresh setting, then the comparison exercise is automatically triggered and we (hopefully) recognise the individual (although connecting name, background, etc. etc. may take a little more time to log and file away!).

This simplification process allows the brain to operate at speeds greatly in excess of even the most powerful computers.

Examples of patterning systems in action

The above discussion has been based around sight, but all senses operate using patterned behaviour:

Notes

Hearing

You pick up a CD that you haven't listened to for a while – or, heaven forfend – you find some old LP's in the loft, with an overwhelming urge to play them. You recognise the cover (you have the image neatly filed away, easily recovered by the brain), but you cannot really remember the associated music other than a very vague recollection.

However, once the music begins to play, and more often as it begins to fade as it comes to the end of a track, the music and words of the next track pop into your mind. Furthermore, you know the music in detail – when the heavy guitars come in etc., and the lyrics flow freely (despite never attempting to learn them!).

The power of patterning systems.

Smell

You are selling your house. A simple trick to play – make sure that there is a fresh pot of coffee on the go plus the smell of freshly bake bread wafting through the house. As the potential buyers cross the threshold – bingo! The smells trigger a "homely" feeling and emotion, and the family fall in love with the new home. Well, sometimes!

The feelings are linked to and can therefore be triggered by smells. The power or patterning systems.

Taste

As an adult, walk into one of those traditional sweetshops and seek out a treat from your youth; curlywurlies, blackjacks, fruit salads, cough candy, liquorice sticks, parma violets... whatever. Tuck in – and reminisce.

Patterning systems in action.

Notes

Touch

It's a simple party game. The host has cleverly constructed a range of cardboard boxes with holes for hands to be inserted. Within each box the wary player will find a delight of some sort waiting – the identify of which must be called based upon touch alone.

Not always a pleasant experience – but a game which is entirely dependent upon patterning systems.

This is all good news. The brain has mastered a data processing trick to allow it to analyse masses of information in real time. However, the same trick represents a very major blockage to creativity.

This is all good news. The brain has mastered a data processing trick to allow it to analyse masses of information in real time. However, the same trick represents a very major blockage to creativity

That "Dopamine Moment"!

De Bono has described the brain as a *self-organised patterning system*. It has evolved mechanisms within the brain for reinforcing this behaviour through the release of the feel-good hormone *dopamine* – providing a kick of pleasure whenever a positive correlation is found between information being processed and a pattern in the brain. The (albeit brief) "kick" is quite profound – responsible for the often audible "Aha!" moment – when suddenly our complete and total understanding emerges from a mass of tangled bits of information – some relevant, some not.

This reinforcement mechanism serves to strengthen the reference pattern, adding credibility and relevance, bringing it to the forefront of the mind.

Notes

Pattern recognition: a major blockage to creativity

With such a patterning system in place within the subconscious to simplify data analysis, the conscious brain is freed up to focus on new objects, for which records of patterns have not been "filed". For example, few of you will have previously seen the image in the figure below. The brain will consequently struggle to analyse it using the subconscious alone, and the conscious mind will be called into play – shutting out all else until the problem is solved (i.e. a pattern is found that neatly links the data – black blobs – together). Assuming you are unfamiliar to the pattern, the brain has no understanding of the relevance of each piece of data – what is relevant, what is not. The subconscious is busy working through your filing system, trying to find a pattern that fits the data. With no clues provided, the challenge is enormous; assumptions are made to simplify the process – perhaps the "black and white"-ness of the image indicates a cow (Friesian?) or a Dalmatian dog?

Eventually, the brain may (or may not) stumble across a stored pattern to make sense of the image. You will know when it hits upon the right interpretation – the image will leap out at you. You may find something which kinda fits – but you just know that you are stretching the stored data in the brain a little too far, and hoping that you are right. Deep down you know that you are wrong – and keep searching.

Figure 3.2: Metaphor for problem solving: black blobs = information (Rupert Sheldrake, 1983)

Notes

Now, whilst the patterning system is an enormous strength in our day-to-day operation, it also represents a significant block to creativity. Such is the strength of the patterning system that the brain will treat a "close match" from the on-board filing cabinet as a "hit". As a consequence, detail from the filing cabinet hit will be transferred to the object, and there will be a tendency to discount any areas of mismatch.

Can you perhaps see a cowboy on a horse?

If you had not previous seen this as the pattern, you may now be surprised – and your brain will go off searching fresh territory within the "filing cabinet", under the headings of "cowboy" and "horse". Many of you will then find it – with an associated "Aha!" moment! Some of you will not; keep searching.

Once you clearly see the image (see end of chapter for those still struggling and by now quite frustrated), a number of interesting things happen:

(i)   The image comes to life – obvious to the eye. Your brain fills in the gaps – using the filing cabinet pattern to complete any missing detail.

(ii)   You discount any information (black splodges) that do not fit with the pattern as clearly irrelevant.

(iii)   Whilst previously you had no difficulty in "not seeing" the image, it is now impossible to let go of. Try <u>*not*</u> seeing the cowboy on a horse.

(iv)   Any other interpretation of the pattern is dismissed, such is the clarity of your (now preferred) "answer".

Notes

This image is a metaphor for an issue within your organisation. Someone is explaining an issue to you, and the black blobs represent pieces of information – some of which are relevant, some of which are not. In finding a pattern you are trying to make sense of the situation. You are drawing upon all of your knowledge, all of your training, all of your past experience to find an interpretation which makes sense of the issue, a pattern which fits the information provided, to then be used as a vehicle for second stage thinking (remember? Gather the information, *process the information (using patterns)*, and then generate a solution).

So, let us consider each of points above these in turn:

(i)   The brain has found a match within its filing system. You see a figure on a horse; given the style of hat on the figure's head, the figure is likely to be *male* and a *cowboy*. Too much analysis; there is not enough information available to determine the sex of the rider, let alone their career choice. But we cannot help ourselves – the brain takes over and fills in the gaps to bring the image to life – all of which merely heightens our belief that we have found the correct interpretation. However, there may be a better interpretation of the pattern, one that can be used to draw better conclusions, and to generate better actions to address the issue. Will the over-processing and filling the gaps prevent us from generating useful ideas? Certainly not. Will it prevent us from generating the best ideas? Absolutely.

(ii)   Information (splodges) that does not fit with the pattern is discounted – treated as irrelevant. I do hope that your pattern is correct! Furthermore, the reverse happens; you will find yourself modifying your interpretation of the facts to make sure that they fit with your pattern. Information can be (*will be*) modified to fit. Will this filtering and potential modification of the information

Notes

prevent us from generating useful ideas? Certainly not. Will it prevent us from generating *creative* ideas? Absolutely.

(iii)   This point is a killer for creativity. Once a pattern is set in place, it is hugely difficult to let go and accept an alternative. Every organisation has "the way that we do things round here" – a patterned behaviour. We understand the wider world around us through patterns – allowing us to make sense of what is happening, patterns which allow us to make decisions. But those patterns are incomplete and imperfect – and so very difficult to change once they have become embedded (remember that Intel jingle? Or McDonalds? Try forgetting it – good luck with that – and then listen to the first 2 notes of the jingle!). Many, many creative problem solving techniques are designed to suspend a particular pattern, taking something that is very, very *familiar* (ingrained!), and trying to make it *unfamiliar*. This process of **making the familiar unfamiliar** will be revisited later. Will this inability to change patterns of understanding prevent us from generating useful ideas? Certainly not. Will it prevent us from generating the <u>*creative*</u> ideas? Absolutely.

(iv)   This ingrained pattern – our interpretation of the facts – becomes fixed. Within an organisational culture, the pattern is shared. It is how we do things around here. If someone then suggests an alternative, something that does not fit with our pattern, then we simply dismiss it – individually or collectively. Simply expressed, it does not fit. We know that the acceptable pattern is based around the cowboy on a horse – and anyone that suggests differently is simply wrong. Will this inability to accept other interpretations, other patterns of understanding prevent us from generating useful ideas? Certainly not. Will it prevent us from generating the <u>*creative*</u> ideas? Absolutely.

Notes

Consider a new member of staff and their first day within the organisation. First days for anyone are disorienting; we have no idea what is going on around us – no pattern to allow us to make sense of things. Without a pattern, we are lost. However, as time goes by we become increasingly comfortable. Colleagues explain how things fit together, and we learn from our own experience. After maybe 4-6 months we get to the stage where we are totally integrated. We have a pattern for the organisation, and with each day that goes by that pattern is affirmed or modified to fit new facts and observations. All is good – we fit in.

However, that pattern of "how we do things around here" is both indelibly inked into our brains, <u>and</u> almost identical to everyone else's pattern within the organisation. If we want to generate *useful ideas*, then this is great; we have a model that can shape our thinking, and whatever we come up with is likely to be consistent with our colleague's thinking.

But if we want to generate something beyond the norm, something that will challenge the conventional wisdom, something creative, then we are instantly in difficulty. To think creatively, to generate something novel, then we need to get rid of the fixed patterns. We need to take the familiar and make it unfamiliar, to free ourselves up, to allow us to seek different interpretations.

By definition, anything which is truly novel will be at odds with conventional thought – not fitting with the ingrained patterns that govern our everyday thinking and consequent behaviour. The tendency is to simply reject the novel idea – on grounds that it simply does not fit with our thinking. Using the "cowboy on a horse" analogy, someone once said that they could see, plain as day, the image of Mount Rushmore within the pattern, with the faces of the US presidents hewn into the rock face.

Notes

Figure 3.3: Mount Rushmore... or a cowboy on a horse? Or simply mad?!

Take a look back at the pattern; any thoughts? The majority (myself included) rapidly conclude that the individual is clearly deluded – verging on madness. How ridiculous – can't he see the cowboy clearly sat upon the horse?

But this is absolutely the wrong reaction for promoting a culture of creativity and innovation. If we reject anything that threatens the integrity of our established patterns, then we will *never* accept novelty – which is so clearly essential within the creative process.

We need to understand the fundamental limitations that patterning places upon our thought processes. Within an organisation, we need to understand this as individuals – but also more broadly across a culture. Unless there is a widespread understanding of the influence of patterning, then novel and useful ideas, great ideas, will wither on the vine. They will be destroyed by the culture – a very major blockage to innovation. (Remember? Innovation = making money/adding value from creative ideas).

Notes

Overcoming the limitations of patterning

The first part of the Creative Problem Solving Cycle (for problem exploration) was introduced in Chapter 2, and now we apply exactly the same cycle of divergent and convergent thinking to the second part – for *Idea Generation*.

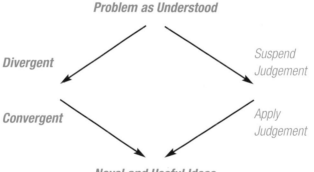

Figure 3.4: Idea Generation Process

Given a problem that has gone through the redefinition process, numerous techniques then exist to effectively structure the Idea Generation process, but in summary:

● The Facilitator will explain the technique that will be used to provoke a process of *divergent thinking*, during which all participants will have little choice other than to suspend judgement. Traditional patterns of thinking will be impossible to apply, and new patterns will emerge – if only as temporary structures to allow fresh thinking the time and space to be explored.

Notes

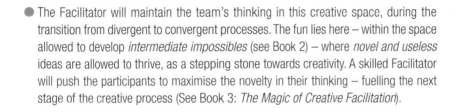

● The Facilitator will maintain the team's thinking in this creative space, during the transition from divergent to convergent processes. The fun lies here – within the space allowed to develop *intermediate impossibles* (see Book 2) – where *novel and useless* ideas are allowed to thrive, as a stepping stone towards creativity. A skilled Facilitator will push the participants to maximise the novelty in their thinking – fuelling the next stage of the creative process (See Book 3: *The Magic of Creative Facilitation*).

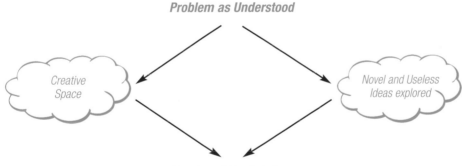

Figure 3.5: The Creative Space

● The focus now shifts towards *convergent thinking*, with judgement allowed to flow back in. However, given too much space the judgement will displace the novelty, which is key to creativity; the key skill of the Facilitator here is to help the group identify the novelty (what makes this idea so special) whilst gradually converting "useless" into "useful". Without this management of the process, the traditional patterns (which, after all, constitute our judgement) will bring their associated baggage of constraints and limitations ("how we do things round here") and creativity is lost.

Notes

- The convergent phase may be somewhat iterative – allowing judgement in, then getting rid to ensure that creativity is not lost, then easing it back in again. This is **the** critical process – and facilitation skills are critical. New patterns are created in the Creative Space, but they are fragile and easy to dispel; great care is required not to destroy them during the convergent process.

- The result will be an idea or concept which should be both novel (the Problem Owner had not thought of **_that_** before) and useful (the Problem Owner is keen to overcome any resistance and make it work).

Figure:3.6: The Cowboy on a horse comes clear (Rupert Sheldrake, 1983)

Notes

Blockage 3:
Mindset

The brain gives us rules that do not exist

When understanding problems and making sense of the information provided, what we hear or read (i.e. what we receive) is not necessarily what our brain takes on board and internalises. It imposes rules which then shut out various solutions – creating blind spots. But of course, and by definition, we do not know that this is happening to us. We need to understand the implications of this *mindset* in order to access better solution/outcomes – to become more creative.

Notes

The previously presented analysis of the brain as a patterning system leads directly into the concept of mindset – a term used to describe a very common consequence of patterning. Mindset will effectively blind an individual to an alternative interpretation of the facts, and is thus a substantial block to creativity. The existing paradigm within an organisation will define a pattern, thereby determining the accepted behaviours, decisions, interpretations etc. Knowledge of this paradigm provides a set of rules which more generally define "how we do things round here".

Consider the "cowboy on a horse" image in Figure 3.2; once the image is clear (Figure 3.6), then the patterning takes over – judgements are made on the relevance of black blobs (information) and those that do not fit the accepted pattern are discarded as irrelevant. Our patterns therefore condition our judgement, and if our patterns (in all of their detailed interpretations) are inaccurate, then mindset will result.

A simple example from school-days is provided below. Nine spots are presented in a simple matrix. With pen on the flat piece of paper, the challenge is to join the nine spots with four straight lines without taking the pen off the paper.

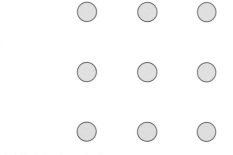

Figure 4.1: Mind Set in action!

Notes

The problem is made difficult because of mind set. The brain communicates the challenge with extra, un-stated, rules, demanding that the four lines are all contained within the nine-dot matrix, or "in the box" formed by the dots. The task is then impossible. The solution is shown at the end of this chapter – and is the origin of the phrase "thinking outside the box".

Any ideas how to solve the same problem with just three straight lines (straight lines, without taking the pen off the paper!)?

Again, the brain gives us rules which do not exist. In this case, having already freed ourselves up and thinking outside the box, the brain has confined us to running through the centre of each spot. It is impossible to solve the problem with this constraint, but the constraint is not real. See solution at end of chapter.

The patterning system of the brain effectively locks into a single way of looking at the problem (whose interpretation will be defined by the pattern which we assign), complete with a set of additional rules and conditions – imposed by the brain.

The above is a very simple example to demonstrate a point, but evidence of mind set is all around us, every day. When someone is sharing an issue, and explaining it in an animated fashion – we hear and see everything, and so should understand perfectly; but our brains are imposing extra conditions which constrain our thinking. These are fed further by our internal patterning behaviour; as the issue is being explained before us, we are frantically trying to find a pattern to help us "understand", to then allow us to use second stage thinking to solve the problem in a logical manner. With this build up of artificial conditioning, the chances of understanding precisely where the other person is coming from are remote. Will we be able to help by generating a useful solution? Probably. Will it be the very best solution? Undoubtedly not (see Figure 2.1).

Notes

Mindset and mental blocks

Each of the artificial blocks to thinking imposed via mindset have a profound effect on our ability to find the very best solutions.

We have a simplistic approach to problem solving, imagining that given an issue that needs to be addressed, we logically scan the entire range of options and select the most appropriate.

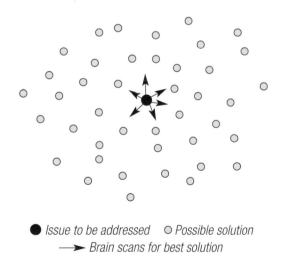

● *Issue to be addressed*   ○ *Possible solution*
⟶ *Brain scans for best solution*

Figure 4.2: The brain scans to find the best possible solution

We imagine that we can "see" all possible solutions, and that we merely select the one that we consider to be "the best".

Notes

However, each bit of mind set places a mental block into our thinking...

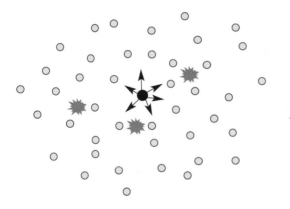

Figure 4.3: We don't know that the mental blocks are getting in the way

...and those blockages effectively hide potential solutions as we scan:

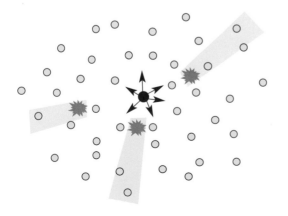

Figure 4.4: And those blocks hide solutions from us – without us knowing

Notes

By definition, we do not know that these blockages exist, and we simply "see" a reduced set of options from which to select. Creativity techniques are simply a vehicle to effectively displace the mental blocks, moving them away from a position embedded within the issue along with its conventional thinking, allowing them then to "see around" the various blockages and to potentially reveal new solutions, which will clearly be novel in the context of the existing paradigm (previously blocked out, so the consequential revelation makes them 'novel').

The situation is somewhat more restricting than above, as the organisational mind set, shared through the culture of the organisation, is then overlaid with the mind set of each individual. Each of us have our own conditioning which has been built up over the years, leading to our own set of individual mental blocks.

The brain is a bucket of sand!
Two colleagues will address or view a problem or opportunity in different ways, each suffering from their own mindset. Any disagreement only serves to enhance the extent of the mindset, creating ever-increasing entrenchment. How can two sane, educated, sensible individuals fail to see each others' point of view? Simple.

> *Imagine the brain to be like a pile of fresh sand, poured out of a bucket and onto the floor, making a little volcano. Imagine that a jug of water hangs over the volcano. The thinking process is akin to pouring the water onto the sand. The water splashes on the top, and then trickles down the side in little rivulets. The result is a crater on the top of the sand, and a series of rivulets down the side of the pile. This represents a single thought process. The rivulets are equivalent to the neural networks that are created within the brain, which allow thought processes to develop.*

Notes

Suppose now that the same thought process is revisited to try to solve the problem again. This is equivalent to another jug of water being poured on to the same pile of sand. The water splashes on the top, and then flows down the side. Most of the water will run down the rivulets that have already been formed, cutting them deeper into the sand. The more that the thought process is repeated, the more entrenched becomes the analysis.

The brain is then effectively constrained into a single way of analysing a problem, or thinking about an opportunity, i.e. mind set is created.

The challenge is to find ways of unlocking the mind set, to break free, and pour out another pile of sand. The vast majority of creative thinking techniques build upon this idea, pouring out a fresh brain, not allowing mind set to condition the thought process. This *sand* analogy is useful to explain the origins of mind set, but we need to dig further into the brain to allow us to understand how we might effectively *re-programme* our thinking, or... to "pour out a fresh brain"!

This leads neatly onto:

Book 2 (An Introduction to Creative Problem Solving Techniques) will introduce mechanisms to overcome those blockages and to embed new behaviours within the organisation;

Book 3 (The Magic of Creative Facilitation) will explain the critical role played by the facilitator within the process of problem solving, distilling the magic and driving new thinking.

Notes

Solutions:

4 Line Trick:

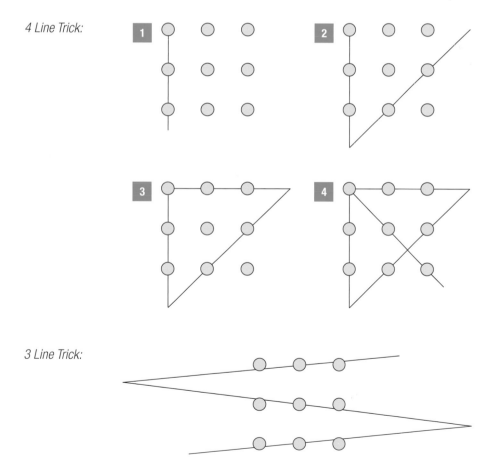

3 Line Trick:

Notes